leap THROUGH TIME

Pyramid

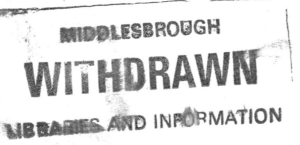

First published in the UK in 2002 by Chrysalis Children's Books,
an imprint of Chrysalis Books Group Plc
The Chrysalis Building, Bramley Road, London W10 6SP
www.chrysalisbooks.co.uk
This paperback edition first published in 2005

Senior Editor: Rasha Elsaeed

Created and produced by Nicholas Harris and Claire Aston,
Orpheus Books Ltd

Text Nicholas Harris
Illustrator Peter Dennis (*Linda Rogers Associates*)
Consultant Dr Jaromir Malek, Director, Griffith Institute, Oxford, England

British Library Cataloguing in Publication Data for this book is available
from the British Library.

ISBN 1 901323 59 5 (hardback)
ISBN 1 84458 432 1 (paperback)

Printed and bound in Malaysia

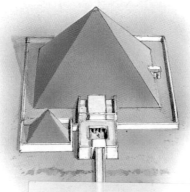

MA	MB	MC
808		
MD	ME	MF
MG	MH	MM
MN	MO	MR
AB	MT	MW

leap THROUGH TIME

Pyramid

illustrated by
Peter Dennis
text by
Nicholas Harris

CHRYSALIS CHILDREN'S BOOKS

Contents

Introduction

Imagine you are in Egypt, thousands of years ago. You are standing on a desert plateau overlooking the mighty river Nile. All around you are thousands of men working hard in the scorching heat of the sun. Many are hauling huge blocks of rock up great ramps, while others are busy chipping away at the stone using mallets and chisels. As the years go by, a massive pyramid takes shape. This immense building will lead a long and eventful life ...

The story told in this book is like a journey. It is not a journey you can make by plane, car or ship. In fact, you don't have to go anywhere at all. You are about to travel through time. With each turn of the page, the date moves forward a few hours, years or even centuries. Each time—every stop on your journey—is like a new chapter in the life of the pyramid. The early days in which it was planned and built, the time when the pharaoh's mummy was entombed inside it, the day, years later, when robbers stole all the treasure from it, the years of neglect—all tell the story of the pyramid.

Look out for a fat man. He appears in all of the illustrations. You can also find a monkey and a vulture on most of the pages too.

Use this thumb index to travel through time! Just find the page you want to see and flip it open. This way you can make a quick comparison between one scene and another, even though some show events that took place some years apart. A little black arrow on the page points to the time of the scene illustrated on that page.

The year 2700 BC

It is early summer in Egypt, along the banks of the river Nile. The great river was in flood until last November. Now the waters have gone away, leaving fertile soil. People work hard in the fields to gather in their crops. The river will flood again in July.

While some harvest emmer wheat and barley, others bring the sheaves to threshing floors. Water, so precious in a

River Nile

Fishing

Cattle

Grain store

Winnowing
(removing husks)

Threshing floor
(where grain is
separated from
stalks)

land where it rarely rains, is taken from the river or specially dug channels. A farmer leads his cattle down to the shore of the Nile to drink, while fishermen gather in their nets. Some hunt wild birds with special sticks.

ANCIENT EGYPT

Egypt is a land in northeastern Africa. It is mostly desert but the River Nile, which flows across it, provides water for crops, animals and people. A great civilization grew up on its banks thousands of years ago. In about 3000 BC, Lower Egypt (the lands near the mouth, or delta, of the Nile) and Upper Egypt (the Nile valley) came under the rule of a single king, or pharaoh.

Hunting birds

Geese

Harvesting wheat

Irrigation channel

Carrying sheaves

Flute player

About 200 years later ...

The ruling pharaoh has already begun to prepare for the end of his life on Earth. He instructs his architect to design a tomb for him that will stand forever. The architect makes plans for a huge pyramid to be built. It is vital that the pyramid's sides face exactly north, south, east and west. A priest observes the rising and setting of stars to fix north precisely.

Since the Land of the Dead is in the west (where the sun sets), the site for building the pyramid is to the west of the Nile, on a high desert plateau. Here, a special ceremony takes place to mark out where the pyramid is to be built. With the pharaoh himself looking on, priests drive stakes into the rocky ground in each of the four corners.

Now the workers get busy to prepare an exactly level site upon which to build up the pyramid. Giant limestone slabs are dragged into place on sledges. Part of the rock on the plateau itself is left to form the inside of the pyramid. Workers use chisels to fit the slabs together.

The pyramid-builders use simple tools to carry out the various jobs. A set square enables right angles to be drawn out or checked. A square level, an A-shaped frame with a weight hanging down from it (a plumb bob), is used to make sure that the ground is exactly level. Copper blades are used to cut and smooth the stone, while mushroom-shaped stones with grooves cut in them guide ropes for pulling heavy loads.

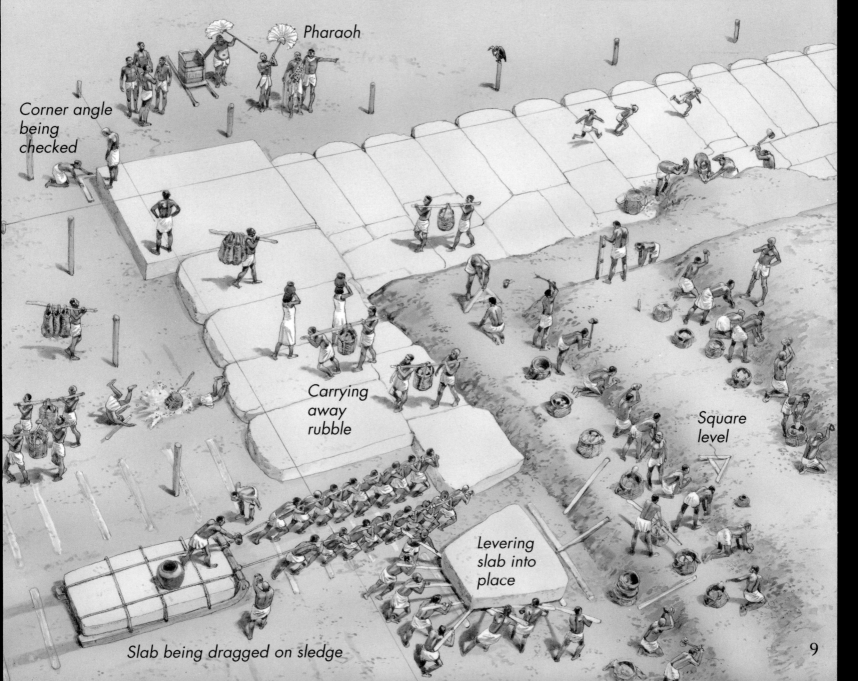

Pharaoh

Corner angle being checked

Carrying away rubble

Square level

Levering slab into place

Slab being dragged on sledge

9

Five years later ...

The building of the new pyramid is in full swing. Workers will later also start to build a small temple (the valley temple) on the banks of the river and a causeway (a covered walkway) leading up to another temple next to the pyramid itself.

Most of the stone used to build the pyramids is quarried from the rocky ground nearby. But fine white limestone for the smooth casing stones comes from Tura, a quarry on the east bank of the Nile. Slabs and columns of granite are brought by boat from Aswan, hundreds of kilometres upriver.

Wood for sledges and general supplies arrive at the building site by boat, where they are unloaded on special jetties. Teams of workers drag sledges, laden with stone, along hauling tracks. It would be difficult to move them across sand, so wooden beams and stone chips are laid on the tracks. They are also covered with wet mud so that the sledges move more easily along them.

Quarry

Reed boat

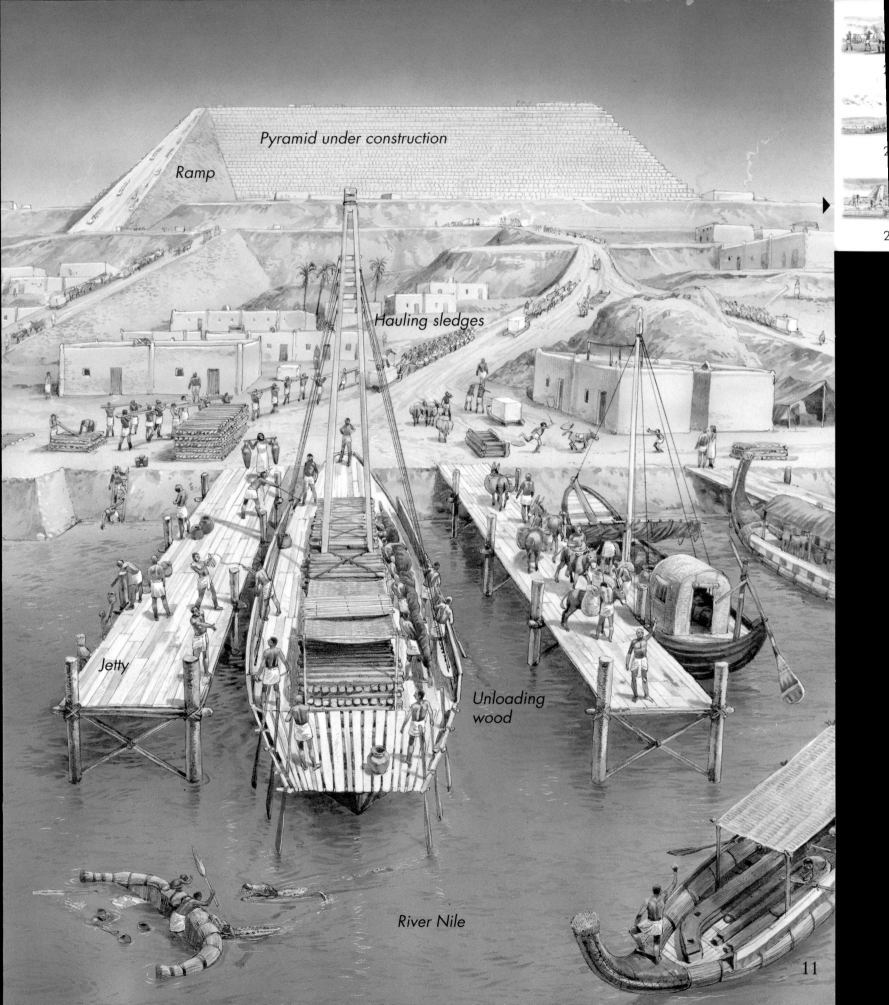

Ramp

Pyramid under construction

Hauling sledges

Jetty

Unloading
wood

River Nile

Ten years later ...

As the pyramid is built higher and higher, an enormous spiral ramp, which winds up all four sides, is built up with it. The ramp provides a hauling track for the blocks of stone to be dragged up to the top. The ramp is built of rubble piled up against the pyramid and held in place by a wall.

It is hard work to drag the heavy stones up the ramps! Workers use levers to help the blocks around corners while others pour water on to the track to smooth the sledges' path.

Ramp

Wall of rubble

Face of pyramid

Moving blocks into position

Levering block

Pouring water on the track

Hauling block

13

2

4

that were
ramids:
square
b bob
under (3)
nisel (4).

Five years later ...

At last, the full height of the pyramid has nearly been completed. The flat area at the top measures only a few metres on each side. It is time to put in place the very highest block of stone: the capstone, sometimes called (because it is itself shaped like a pyramid) the pyramidion. After a ceremony of prayers to the gods, this special stone, carved out of hard granite, is dragged up the spiral ramp and levered into place.

Now the work to shave away the rough edges of the casing stones begins. Chiselmen work from scaffolding, while others polish the flat stone faces until they are smooth and shine in the sun. Finally the pyramid is painted red, while the pyramidion is covered with a thin layer of gold.

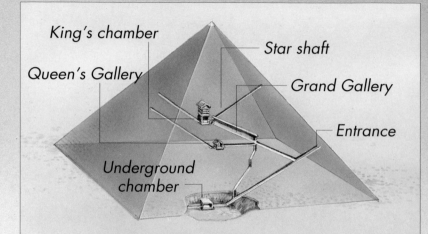

King's chamber
Queen's Gallery
Star shaft
Grand Gallery
Entrance
Underground chamber

INSIDE THE PYRAMID

While the pyramid was being built, chambers and passages inside it were also being constructed. The builders positioned the blocks forming the roofs of these spaces so that they could support the enormous weight of the pyramid above them. This illustration shows the inside of the Great Pyramid of Khufu.

Removing ramp

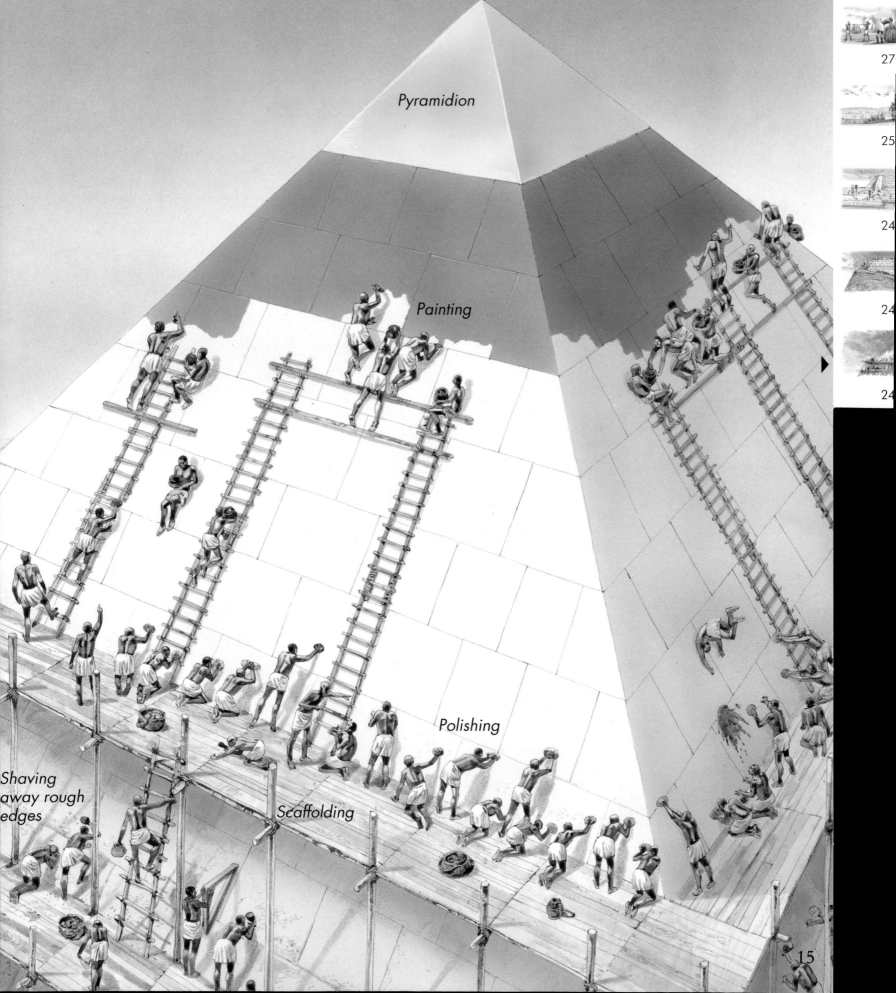

Pyramidion

Painting

Polishing

Scaffolding

Shaving
away rough
edges

Seven years later ...

Temple

Valley
temple

view of a
d, with its
useway.

The pharaoh has died. To the Egyptians, his death marks the beginning of a new life in another world. His funeral and burial in the pyramid is the first stage on this voyage to the Afterlife.

The pharaoh's body must first be prepared for burial. It is cleansed, by removing its organs such as the liver, lungs and stomach, and preserved by being turned into a mummy—wrapped in bandages. This process, carried out by the embalmers (the men responsible for preserving the body), will take about two months to complete.

The mummy is then placed in a coffin and carried on a royal funerary barge along the Nile to the pyramid. Thousands of people watch the procession from the river bank. Travelling with the coffin are mourners, members of the pharaoh's family, priests and priestesses, and the treasures that will be buried with him in his tomb.

The barge draws alongside the valley temple and the pharaoh's mummified body is taken inside.

Valley temple

Pyramid

Temple

Causeway

Royal funerary barge

Coffin

River Nile

Side of barge cut
away so we can
see inside

2700 BC

2500 BC

2495 BC

2485 BC

2480 BC

2473 BC

To prepare the mummy, the embalmers first removed the organs from the body. Then an embalmer dressed as the god Anubis wrapped the body in bandages.

A few hours later ...

The mummy is taken to a large hall in the valley temple. Here a ceremony called the "opening of the mouth" is performed. Its purpose is to allow the dead pharaoh to breathe, eat and speak in the Afterlife.

A priest dressed as the jackal-headed god Anubis (the god responsible for mummifying bodies) holds the mummy upright while another performs the ceremony, holding out an adze (a kind of hand tool).

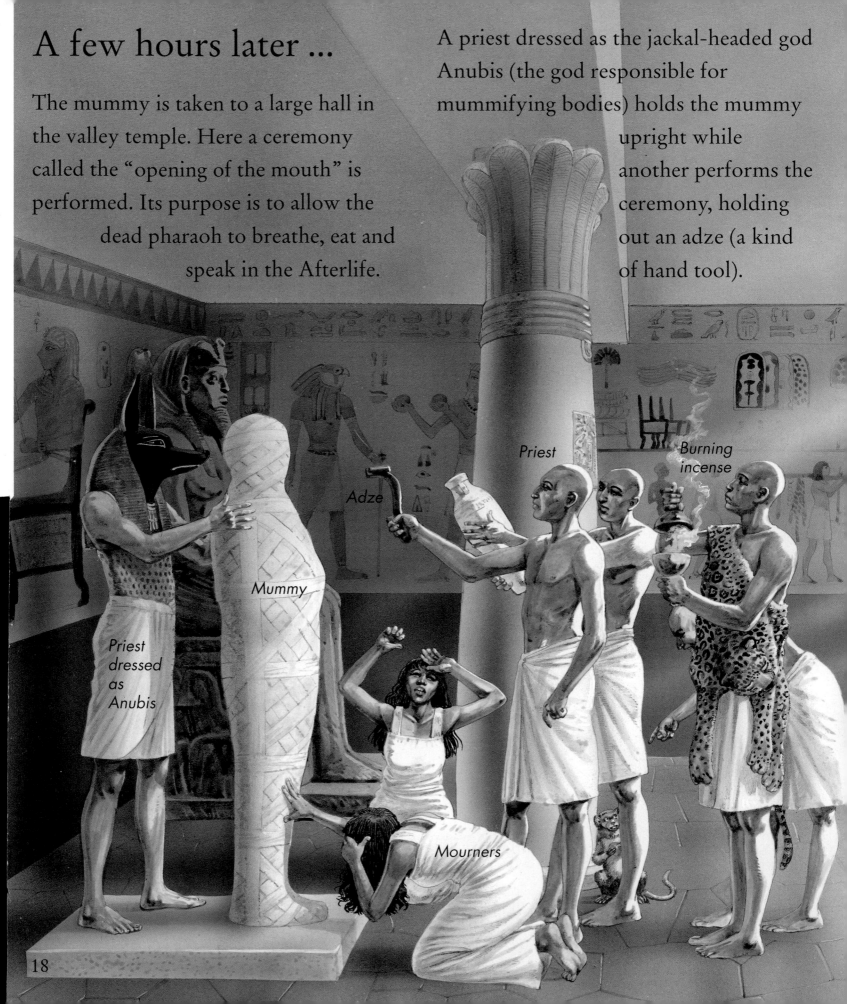

Adze

Priest

Burning incense

Mummy

Priest dressed as Anubis

Mourners

The mummy is then placed in a wooden coffin and taken to the pyramid itself. Priests carry the coffin along a narrow passage to the burial chamber. There they lower it into a sarcophagus, a coffin made of stone. Canopic jars, containing the pharaoh's internal organs, are placed beside it.

Food, furniture, jewellery and other things the pharaoh will need in the Afterlife, are left in the chamber. Then the priests leave. Granite blocks seal off the chamber. On the outside of the pyramid, a final casing stone is levered into place, concealing the entrance—the priests hope—forever.

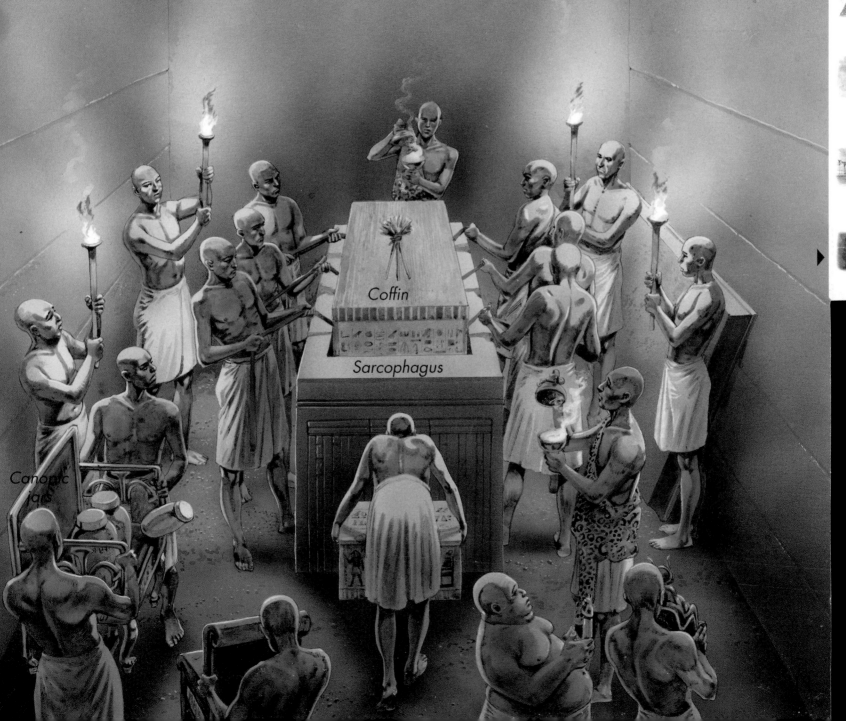

Coffin

Sarcophagus

Canopic jars

2700 BC

2500 BC

2495 BC

2485 BC

2480 BC

2473 BC

A few hours later

The ancient Egyptians believed people had more than one soul. The *ka* was the "life force", kept alive by food. It is often shown in Egyptian art by upraised arms.

The *ba* was someone's "personality". It was pictured as a human-headed bird.

The *akh* was a person's "shining spirit". It was shown as a crested ibis.

Pyramid

Fifty years later...

The pharaoh's remains have remained undisturbed inside his pyramid for years. His divine spirit has, the ancient Egyptians believe, joined the gods in heaven. But to keep his "life force" alive priests carry out daily

Priests

Bread

services in which offerings of food and drink are made to his spirit.

Priests lead a procession to a temple built against the side of the pyramid. Here there is a stela (a gravestone) and statues of the pharaoh. Some priests offer loaves of bread, bowls of wine, milk or water, and various fruit and vegetables on an altar in front of the stela. Others offer bowls of blood and meat from slaughtered bulls.

Clothes

Courtyard of mortuary temple

2700 BC

2500 BC

2495 BC

2485 BC

2480 BC

2473 BC

A few hours later

2423 BC

In later years, pyramids were no longer built in Egypt. Pharaohs were buried instead in tombs cut in the Valley of the Kings. One of the most famous was that of Tutankhamun. His burial chamber was discovered in 1922 full of treasures.

Tutankhamun, whose likeness we know from this gold mask found on his mummy, is called the Boy King. Objects from his tomb tell us a lot about ancient Egypt.

About three hundred years later...

Thieves have broken into the burial chamber. Somehow they have discovered the concealed entrance to the pyramid and the passageway leading to the burial chamber. Finding their way barred by the granite slabs, they have dug their own tunnel to reach the tomb, where they knock through the walls. They find the jewellery, the furniture and the other treasures left in the burial chamber.

Using mallets and levers they prise the lid off the sarcophagus. Everything, including even the mummy itself, is taken away.

TROUBLED TIMES

By about 2200 BC, the Old Kingdom of ancient Egypt was in trouble. Priests and local governors had become more powerful, while the pharaoh's power had become weaker. At the same time, a great drought may have struck Egypt, ruining harvests. As the kingdom collapsed, violence and famine took hold. All the pyramids were looted.

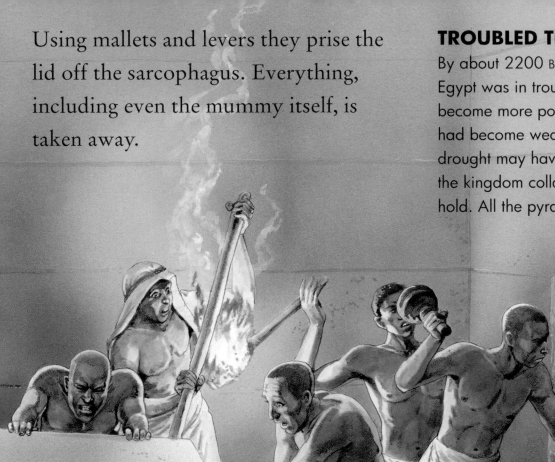

2700 BC

2500 BC

2495 BC

2485 BC

2480 BC

2473 BC

A few hours later

2423 BC

2120 BC

23

The ancient Egyptians wrote in picture signs, using several different scripts: hieroglyphs, detailed pictures for inscriptions on walls and monuments *(above)*, hieratic, a shortened form for everyday purposes, and demotic, a later, even shorter, form.

One of the few treasures of the pyramids not stolen or destroyed was this stone statue of Khafre, whose pyramid is one of the three famous Giza pyramids. It was discovered in a valley temple.

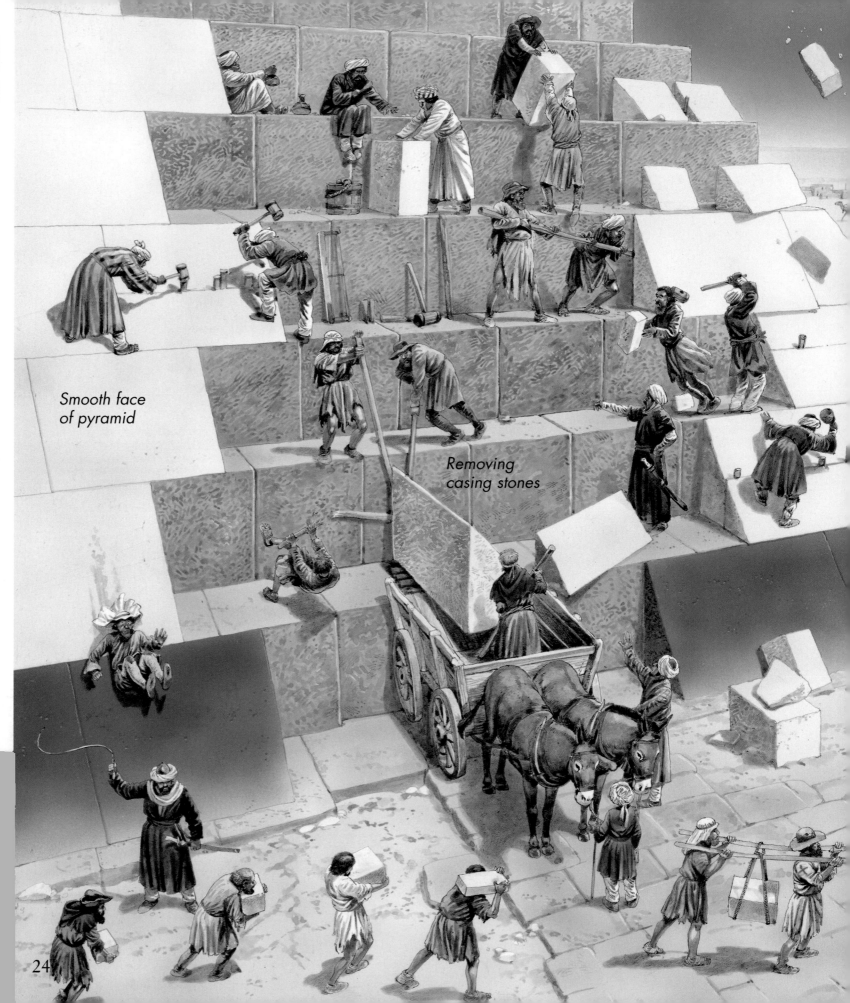

Smooth face of pyramid

Removing casing stones

24

About three thousand years later...

The ancient Egyptian civilization has vanished. Drifting sands from the desert have built up around many pyramids. Some have collapsed in a heap of rubble.

Egypt is now under the rule of the Arabs, who conquered it in AD 642. With no-one alive who can understand hieroglyphic script, the Arabs make up their own legends about why the pyramids were built...

In the search for treasure that they think is hidden inside the pyramids, some adventurers break into passages inside the pyramids. But for many people the monuments are useful for one thing only: building stone. Some smaller pyramids are destroyed. Others have smooth casing stones that can be used for constructing new houses and palaces. Workers are ordered to chisel it off and take it away to new building sites.

Supervisor

Arab ruler

2700 BC

2500 BC

2495 BC

2485 BC

2480 BC

2473 BC

A few hours later

2423 BC

2120 BC

AD 800

A thousand years later...

It is the year 1798. Napoleon Bonaparte, France's great leader, has conquered a vast empire in Europe. Now he has decided to take control of Egypt. He has led his soldiers to attack Cairo, capital of Egypt. The Mamelukes, rulers of Egypt for the past 500 years, are set to stop him. Their army meets the French army near the pyramids of Giza. Napoleon says to his men before the battle begins: "Soldiers, forty centuries look down upon you from these pyramids."

The French scholars who visited Egypt during Napoleon's conquest wrote about their finds in the *Description de L'Égypte*. Later visitors took away many treasures, before proper archaeological excavations were begun in the late 19th century.

The Rosetta Stone was a vital help to historians in the understanding of ancient Egyptian writing. Because its inscriptions were written in Greek as well as hieroglyphic and demotic scripts, Frenchman Jean-François Champollion was able to crack the code of hieroglyphic writing in 1824.

French soldiers

Mameluke soldiers

French soldiers

26

The Mameluke soldiers put up a brave fight, but they are no match for the well-organized French army. They are easily defeated at the "Battle of the Pyramids". Napoleon is the new ruler of Egypt—but only until British forces destroy the French fleet later that year.

THE FIRST EUROPEAN DISCOVERIES

European scholars first visited the pyramids in the 17th century. They found the great monuments mostly stripped of their smooth casing stones. The burial chambers inside the pyramids were empty.

Scholars also accompanied Napoleon on his expedition. They made maps and engravings, and collected an enormous amount of valuable information about ancient Egypt. French scholars also discovered the Rosetta Stone (opposite).

2700 BC

2500 BC

2495 BC

2485 BC

2480 BC

2473 BC

A few hours later

2423 BC

2120 BC

AD 800

1798

Pyramids

French soldiers

Mameluke soldiers

The first pyramid in ancient Egypt, the Step Pyramid of Saqqara, was built by Imhotep, architect to King Djoser in around 2650 BC. It was surrounded by walls and other buildings and courtyards. The steps, it was once said, are a kind of staircase to the stars.

Early pyramid builders did not always get the shape right! Halfway up, they decided the angle was too steep, so they changed it to a gentler slope. The Bent Pyramid was the result.

All later pyramids had four straight sides, perhaps representing the Sun's rays shining down on the pharaoh. Three giant pyramids were built at Giza by Khufu, his son Khafre *(above)* and grandson Menkaure.

Today

The plateau on the west bank of the Nile is busy. Tourists from all over the world have come here to see the pyramids. Many gaze in awe at their sheer size. The biggest pyramids are still among the largest buildings ever created.

Local people are only too happy to help tourists part with their money! Everywhere there are kiosks selling souvenirs and camel rides on offer. Local guides are also on hand to inform people about the monuments. Maybe some visitors are wondering about how the pyramids were built, many years ago ...

EGYPT'S TOURISTS

Ever since Napoleon's conquest, many travellers, scholars and tourists have visited Egypt to marvel at its great monuments. A lot of treasures were taken from Egypt and can still be found on display in museums around the world. Towards the end of the 19th century, hotels were built. But with the huge increase of air travel in the last 30 years, the tourism business in Egypt expanded greatly. People arrive from all over the world to visit the pyramids, temples and museums and go on cruises down the Nile.

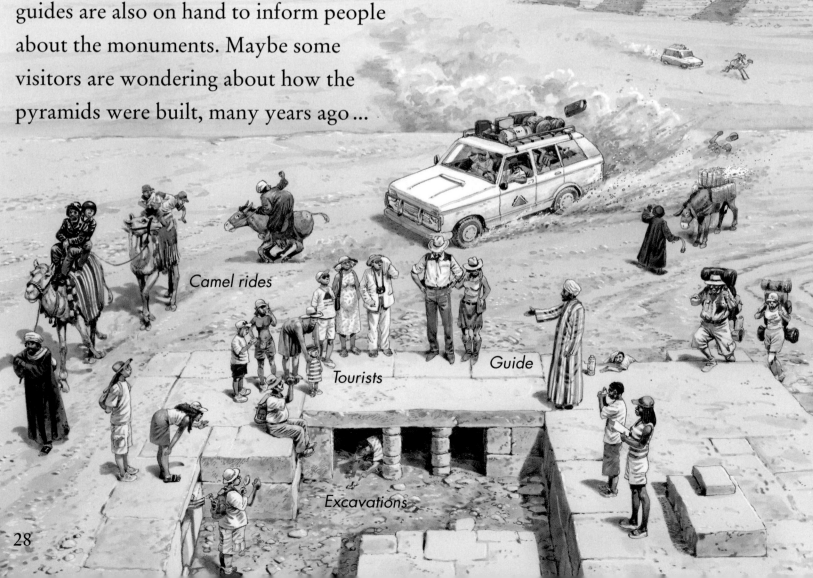

Camel rides

Tourists

Guide

Excavations

Hot-air balloon

Pyramids

Camel rides

Souvenir sellers

Tourists

2700 BC

2500 BC

2495 BC

2485 BC

2480 BC

2473 BC

A few hours later

2423 BC

2120 BC

AD 800

1798

Today

Glossary

Adze A tool with a blade set at right angles to the handle. A ceremonial adze was used in the "opening of the mouth" *(see page 18)*.

Afterlife Life after death.

Akh To the ancient Egyptians, the soul of a dead person that has been reborn in the Afterlife. The word means "shining spirit".

Architect Someone who designs buildings.

Ba An ancient Egyptian word for someone's personality. The *ba* had the ability to eat, drink and travel in the Afterlife. But it could not function if the dead body decayed.

Canopic jar A container in which the organs removed from a dead body were stored before mummification took place.

Capstone The pyramid-shaped stone at the very top of the pyramid.

Casing stones The outer layer of a pyramid, usually made from fine limestone. The casing stones were smoothed, polished and painted.

Causeway The covered way that led from a pyramid's valley temple to another temple next to the pyramid itself. The inside walls were often highly decorated.

Civilization A people who have developed laws, trade, arts, monuments and other aspects of a settled way of life.

Demotic The normal, everyday writing used by the Egyptians in the later years of their civilization.

Embalm To preserve a dead body from decay.

Emmer A type of wheat grown in ancient Egypt.

Hieratic The normal, everyday form of writing used by ancient Egyptians.

Hieroglyphs A form of writing, using signs resembling pictures, on walls and monuments.

Incense A material that gives off fragrant fumes when burnt. It is used on ceremonial occasions.

Ka To the ancient Egyptians, a person's life force or "double". When kept alive by food offerings, it ensured a person would be reborn into the Afterlife.

Mummification The process of embalming—and so preserving—a body, by removing the organs, drying it out, then wrapping it in linen bandages.

Pharaoh Another name for the kings of ancient Egypt.

Plumb bob A heavy weight hung on a string to show an exactly vertical line.

Pyramidion Another word for capstone.

Resin A sticky substance that comes from the sap of trees and is used for embalming.

Sarcophagus The outer stone coffin in which a wooden coffin was laid.

Stela A slab or stone with inscriptions carved on it.

Index